CW00692850

MAKING THE
MOST OF THE
CROSS

JOHN CHAPMAN

MAKING THE MOST OF THE CROSS

JOHN CHAPMAN

Making the Most of the Cross
© Matthias Media 2011

Matthias Media
(St Matthias Press Ltd. ACN 067 558 365)
PO Box 225
Kingsford NSW 2032
Australia
Telephone: (02) 9663 1478; international: +61-2-9663-1478
Facsimile: (02) 9663 3265; international: +61-2-9663-3265
Email: info@matthiasmedia.com.au
Internet: www.matthiasmedia.com.au

Matthias Media (USA)
Telephone: 330 953 1702; international: +1-330-953-1702
Facsimile: 330 953 1712; international: +1-330-953-1712
Email: sales@matthiasmedia.com
Internet: www.matthiasmedia.com

Scripture quotations are from The Holy Bible, English Standard Version® (ESV®), copyright © 2001 by Crossway, a publishing ministry of Good News Publishers. Used by permission. All rights reserved.

ISBN 978 1 921896 00 2

All rights reserved. Except as may be permitted by the Copyright Act, no part of this publication may be reproduced in any form or by any means without prior permission from the publisher.

Cover design and typesetting by Lankshear Design.

DEDICATED TO
Map Vreeken, fellow traveller and friend,
and all my other friends from the Bible study group at
Donald Robinson Village.

Contents

Preface

"I HAVE ALREADY HAD MY 76TH BIRTHDAY." So began *Making the Most of the Rest of Your Life*. In that book I explored with you what life after death in the new creation would be like. I did this so that we would look forward to it and not be afraid of dying.

Well, I'm now a few months past 80 and I am still going. I have lost a couple of specialists (which may seem careless) and acquired some new ones. It is one thing to look with longing at the new creation, but I still have to live in the here and now with my frail body.

At Easter I was struck all over again by the importance of the death and resurrection of the Lord Jesus. The freedom to marvel afresh at what Jesus did for us is a great gift. The more I think about it, the better it becomes, and I decided I had to write about it.

Although it is possible to describe the death and resurrection of Jesus as if they are two events, they are really describing two aspects of the same event. This event is at the heart of what Jesus came to do. It is central to the Lord Jesus' thinking, and it should be central to our thinking.

While we are waiting to take our place in the new creation, Jesus' death and resurrection should be at the heart of what we do. This event needs to govern our love for God and the way we treat other people. It is easy to believe it happened and yet let it slip from its rightful place in our lives.

In writing this short book, I want to help us reassess our thinking about this great event. I hope you enjoy reading the book as much as I have enjoyed writing it.

John Chapman
February 2011

Introduction: *The* event in human history

EVERY NOW AND THEN, HUMANITY witnesses a history-changing event. Something happens that affects how people live—like the invention of the wheel or the discovery of penicillin. Sometimes these events change how people view the world. World War II made us deeply suspicious of authority. 9/11 made us suspicious of religious zealots.

In calling my introduction '*The* event in human history', I am not referring to any of these events, but to the death and resurrection of Jesus of Nazareth in the first century AD. The most zealous of all religious zealots died and then rose to become the ruler of the world. This was the ultimate history-changing event, and there has been none like it before or since.

How can I make such a claim? It is because this event is the means by which God has reconciled the world to himself. It is the only means by which our sins can be forgiven. Nothing is more important than it. From Jesus' point of view, nothing he achieved was greater than his death and resurrection. He said:

> "For this reason the Father loves me, because I lay down my life that I may take it up again. No-one takes it from me, but I lay it down of my own accord. I have authority

to lay it down, and I have authority to take it up again. This charge I have received from my Father." (John 10:17-18)

Did you notice how, as Jesus looks at his relationship with his Father, he speaks as though the Father loves him only because of his coming death and resurrection? What a wonderful declaration! Jesus sees his death and resurrection for us as central even to his relationship with his Father.

There is no doubt that the death and resurrection of the Lord Jesus Christ is at the centre of all God's activities, and there are two reasons why we need to understand it.

Firstly, it is impossible to make any sense of what the Bible is saying if we fail to understand this event. The entire Bible hinges on it, because it's the only thing that explains the apparent contradiction between a *loving* God and a *just* God.

Think about that for a minute. In the pages of Scripture we are presented with the God who loves the world. At the same time, he is passionate about truth and righteousness. He loves justice and will see that it is done in his world—and so the guilty will be punished.

These two ideas seem to be in direct conflict with each other. How can God love people and yet relegate them to hell? How can God love the wicked and punish them at the same time?

Some people have suggested to me that God's love will override his other attributes and all will be well in the end. This sounds fine until you think through the implications. If this is the case, then what does God think about my sin? Does he say, "Let's skip it, John"? Does he do the same for your sin? It sounds like a wonderful idea.

But does God say that for the six million who went through the gas chambers of Auschwitz and Belzec? Does

God say to their murderers, "Let's skip it"? Does it matter if there is no justice for those who died? If God says, "Let's skip it", he is turning his back on the evil that touched and affected them. Does God cease to love these victims of human sin? Does he only love the perpetrators? Ignoring the sin of the perpetrators is to ignore the evil done to the victims.

This solution is horrific in its implications. It is hardly loving! It means that there is no real difference between the death of a dog and the death of six million people in the gas chambers. God does not care enough to seek justice in either case. If God will not act justly when faced with the death of six million people, then it really does not matter what we do or what is done to us. God will ignore it all. If God does not care about anything we do or anything that happens to us, then ultimately our lives have no meaning.

Mercifully, the Bible takes a totally different point of view. Life is not meaningless. Truth and justice, mercy and love will prevail. The death of Jesus says so! In the death of Jesus on the cross, God does not say, "Let's skip it!" Indeed, the cross shows that God loves us enough to seek justice.

The second reason we need to understand Jesus' death and resurrection is that it is possible for us to so emphasize the justice and righteousness of God that it dwarfs his love. I used to attend a church where the teaching was much like this. I remember one night after church a friend said to me, "I agree with everything he says, but just sometimes I would like him to tell me that God loves me!" The only way to avoid this lack of balance is to focus on the death and resurrection of the Lord Jesus.

Sometimes the circumstances of life may cause us to

wonder if God has forgotten us. Everything seems to be going wrong. But the death of the Lord Jesus is above our circumstances. Nothing can take away the fact that Christ died for us. No matter what happens to you or to me, the death of the Lord Jesus says, "I love you". Nothing can change that. Be in no doubt that God loves you. Jesus' death remains as a beacon of God's eternal love for us.

～

IN THE REST OF THIS BOOK I WILL explore the many facets of the death and resurrection of the Lord Jesus, and show how the Lord Jesus and the apostles understood this event and the significance of it. I will show you *how* this event brings together God's justice and God's love. I will describe the different ways the Bible sees the importance of the death and resurrection, and at the end of each section I will suggest a prayer that you might like to pray.

If you have not yet put your trust in the Lord Jesus Christ, my prayer is that you will think about the work of Christ on your behalf, and enter into the Christian life; that you will revel with those of us who already believe at the marvellous love God has for us.

PART I
THE DEATH OF
THE LORD JESUS

1 | Jesus' death brings salvation

> The saying is trustworthy and deserving of full acceptance, that Christ Jesus came into the world to save sinners, of whom I am the foremost. (1 Timothy 1:15)

THE TITLE 'SAVIOUR' OR 'RESCUER' is often given to the Lord Jesus in Scripture (John 4:42; Acts 13:23; 1 Thessalonians 1:10; Titus 1:4; 2 Peter 1:11; 1 John 4:14). God wants us to understand that we can't make any sense of who Jesus is if we fail to put salvation at the heart of what Jesus is on about.

Before Jesus was born, the angel said to Joseph (the engaged partner of Mary, the mother of Jesus), "She will bear a son, and you shall call his name Jesus, for he will save his people from their sins" (Matthew 1:21). The name 'Jesus' means 'God brings salvation'. Salvation is so central to Jesus' mission that it is part of his name.

When Jesus was born in Bethlehem, the angels announced to the shepherds:

> "Fear not, for behold, I bring you good news of great joy that will be for all the people. For unto you is born this day in the city of David a Saviour, who is Christ the Lord." (Luke 2:10-11)

The key thing the angels declare when they proclaim his birth is the fact that Jesus is a saviour.

John's Gospel reminds us that "God did not send his Son into the world to condemn the world, but in order that the world might be saved through him" (John 3:17). John tells us that saving the world is the entire reason Jesus was sent into the world by God.

The fact that Jesus is the saviour of the world implies that the world needs to be saved or rescued. You don't send a lifeguard into the ocean when no-one is drowning. And when we ask the question, "From what do we need to be rescued?" the Bible's answer is clear. We need to be saved from "the wrath to come" (1 Thessalonians 1:10).

This is a familiar theme for those who are Bible readers. God's wrath is described in the Bible in several ways. In the first chapter of his letter to the Romans, Paul argues that God's wrath is already being felt in the world as God lets sinful people loose on each other (Romans 1:18-32). In this chapter, the phrase "God gave them up" is used again and again to show that God expresses his wrath by handing sinful people over to their sinfulness (see verses 24, 26 and 28). And we don't need to look very far to see the evidence. The 20th century will go down in history as a great example of how people can prey on each other in our world. It can be scary to live in a world where "might is right" and the weak are at the mercy of the strong.

However, the term "the wrath to come" is also used of God's final judgement. This is the judgement that will occur when God brings an end to the history of this world and introduces what the Bible calls "the new creation".

When the apostle Paul is writing to the Thessalonians, he commends them for the response they made to the gospel. He describes their response in a way that draws our attention to the significance of the final judgement:

For they themselves report concerning us the kind of reception we had among you, and how you turned to God from idols to serve the living and true God, and to wait for his Son from heaven, whom he raised from the dead, Jesus who delivers us from the wrath to come. (1 Thessalonians 1:9-10)

The Thessalonians showed true repentance and faith. That was the right response to the gospel.

Firstly, they repented of following the wrong gods. When Paul preached that the true God was the God and Father of Jesus Christ, they believed him. They then needed to stop worshipping their idols. They needed to say, "We have been wrong in this practice". Some may have been mistaken, others may have worshipped the wrong gods wilfully; but whatever they had been doing, they now turned their backs on the idols and turned to the living God to serve him absolutely.

It was genuine repentance, and it was matched with genuine faith. Paul had told them about the death of Jesus. He had explained that Jesus took the punishment their sins deserved and that they could be forgiven by trusting in his death. The Thessalonians did so and were now waiting "for his Son from heaven, whom he raised from the dead, Jesus who delivers us from the wrath to come". They had abandoned any hope that all would be well because of their track record. They knew they were rightly condemned, and they were glad to have a rescuer. They believed that Jesus was their saviour and they trusted him to save them from the wrath to come. They had a genuine faith in Jesus.

From this we can see that those who trust in Jesus will be forgiven. Those who reject his offer of forgiveness will be punished, as they deserve (John 3:18). Jesus has taken the full punishment for the sins of the world (1 John 2:2). If we trust him, he freely forgives us and so rescues us from the judgement to come.

One night when I was speaking at Oxford University, I spoke on the coming judgement. After the meeting a young lady came to me, white with rage. She announced, "I hate people who try and frighten you into the kingdom". During the conversation I said, "The question isn't 'Have I tried to frighten you?' but 'Is there anything to be frightened about?'" We would be fools if there were something we really should be frightened about and we took no effort to avoid it.

For Christians, this salvation is the source of endless joy. It is described in the Bible in several ways. We have been saved from the penalty of sin (Romans 8:1), we will be saved from the presence of sin (1 Thessalonians 1:10), and we are being saved day by day from the power of sin (Galatians 5:16). All this was achieved for us when Jesus took our place as he died on the cross.

When I talk about 'sin', I am not talking about some slight imperfection in our characters. Most of us know we are not perfect, but many do not recognize that sin is more deep-seated in us than merely a minor blemish. At heart, we are rebels to the idea that God should rule our wills. We argue with God. We disregard his word when we do not agree with it. We choose to do wrong when we know the right. As God is genuinely and truly good, it is a terrible thing to oppose his will. When we do this, as we do regularly, we are siding with evil and against good. We need forgiveness.

It was no simple matter to take away the sin of the world, and it was of the greatest importance. We can see this by looking at Jesus' attitude to his forthcoming death on the cross. He cried, "My Father, if it be possible, let this cup pass from me; nevertheless, not as I will, but as you will" (Matthew 26:39).

Jesus' prayer was answered with an emphatic "No", so we can be sure that the cross was the only way to deal with our sin. There was no other way. The Lord Jesus died for us. This was a great act of self-sacrificial love. And it was a great act of the Father's love in sending Jesus to die.

This should fill us with wonder and love.

A suggested prayer

Lord Jesus, thank you for the great salvation that you earned for us.

2 | Jesus' death is a substitute

> He himself bore our sins in his body on the tree, that we might die to sin and live to righteousness. By his wounds you have been healed. (1 Peter 2:24)

IN THIS LETTER, PETER IS USING the death of the Lord Jesus as an example of endurance under persecution. Almost in passing, he tells us that Jesus substituted himself for us when he died on the cross. Jesus bore *our* sins when he hung on the tree. This is an important aspect of our understanding of what Jesus did when he died on the cross.

The Bible tells us that the punishment for sin is death—that is, separation from God (Romans 6:23). When human beings die, we die as punishment for a life lived in rebellion against God. But Jesus died in our place, and so took the punishment that we deserve. This enables God to forgive those who place their trust in his Son.

The writer to the Hebrews is at pains to tell us that the Lord Jesus had no sins of his own:

> For we do not have a high priest who is unable to sympathize with our weaknesses, but one who in every respect has been tempted as we are, yet without sin. (Hebrews 4:15)

The Lord Jesus is without sin. He was tempted just like we are, but—of all men and women—he alone never gave into temptation; he never disobeyed God, even a little bit. He lived in obedience to God all his life and so was well qualified to make a perfect sacrifice. Indeed, his sacrifice is unique, unrepeatable and sufficient for all who turn to him.

> For it was indeed fitting that we should have such a high priest, holy, innocent, unstained, separated from sinners, and exalted above the heavens. He has no need, like those high priests, to offer sacrifices daily, first for his own sins and then for those of the people, since he did this once for all when he offered up himself. (Hebrews 7:26-27)

Jesus made a sacrifice once for all time and for all people. He did not die for *his* sins (for he had none); his death was a perfect sacrifice for *our* sins. When Jesus died on the cross, he took upon himself the full weight of the punishment due for the sins of the world. He died instead of us. He substituted himself for us by dying the death that we deserve. And that death he died is sufficient for each one of us—for me and for you. We no longer need to be punished for our sins, and Jesus is able to forgive those who put their faith in him.

In another part of the Bible his death is described prophetically like this:

> Surely he has borne our griefs
> and carried our sorrows;
> yet we esteemed him stricken,
> smitten by God, and afflicted.
> But he was wounded for our transgressions;
> he was crushed for our iniquities;

upon him was the chastisement that brought us peace,
   and with his stripes we are healed.
All we like sheep have gone astray;
   we have turned—every one—to his own way;
and the LORD has laid on him
   the iniquity of us all. (Isaiah 53:4-6)

The prophet Isaiah sees the servant of God bearing the sins of the world. The servant does this by taking my punishment and yours. The prophet is speaking about the Lord Jesus, declaring ahead of time why his death on the cross was so important. Jesus' death was a sin-bearing death. He took the punishment that we deserve for our sins. He bore the griefs and carried the sorrows that are the natural consequence of our sins. He took the wounds that we should take. This is what it means to say that "the iniquity of us all" was laid upon him.

Some have argued that this is immoral. To this day, some say they cannot become Christians because of this fact. But by what standard of morality should we judge God? He is the author of morality. It is part of the extraordinary blindness of human beings that we act as though we are God's equals. We make demands of God and seek to apply our moral rules to him, as though we were his equals. We are not. None of us is the Creator, and we have no right to define how he must behave towards us. He is God and we are not. We are his creatures, nothing more. God makes demands of us and establishes limits for how we are to live *because* he made us. We do not do that for our Creator.

That being said, we are familiar with the idea of people substituting themselves by taking the punishment of others. For example, parents often pay the fines of their children. No-one seems to think this is immoral. Sometimes people have even given their lives so that others could stay alive. I was brought up to believe this was heroic. In light of this, it is hard to see what complaint people might have about the Lord Jesus taking our punishment because of his great love for us.

More often, people say that God is wrong to be satisfied by Jesus dying in our place; that somehow it is immoral for God to allow Jesus to take our place and bear our sins. However, God is the offended party. He is the only one who can see what satisfies him, and he has said the death of the Lord Jesus is sufficient. Is it really immoral for God to allow a substitution to take place, or even to arrange for one on our behalf?

It is all too easy to misrepresent this doctrine and depict God the Father as a vindictive child-abuser who punished his innocent Son by forcing him to suffer for things he never did. However, the Bible knows nothing of this travesty. The Father loved the Son and he loved the world. The Son loved us and gave himself for us. In the Godhead there was no disagreement about the plan of salvation. They were totally of one mind on this matter. The Father did not force any punishment upon the Son; the Son himself chose to bear it on our behalf because of his love for us. This is anything but child abuse!

This is an example of love, unmatched by any other event in history. In some mysterious way that is hidden from us, there was a fracture in the Godhead. The Son of God was separated from the Father when he bore the sin of the world. And the Father and the Son took this action together, because they loved us.

Without the death of the Lord Jesus for us we would

have to bear the punishment for our own sins and there could be no forgiveness at all. Our prospects would be very grim indeed, but because of Jesus' death in our place we can be at peace with God. What a wonderful truth this is.

Another part of the Bible describes it like this:

> For our sake he made him to be sin who knew no sin, so that in him we might become the righteousness of God. (2 Corinthians 5:21)

Jesus bore our sins, substituting himself for each one of us. Because of his death in our place, we can be forgiven and accepted by God as righteous.

It was a great act of the Father's love to allow the Son to die in our place (John 3:16). This should fill us with wonder and praise.

A suggested prayer

Lord Jesus, your love overwhelms me. Thank you for making salvation available to me through your death in my place. Help me to love you more and more.

3 | Jesus' death is a ransom

"For even the Son of Man came not to be served but to serve, and to give his life as a ransom for many." (Mark 10:45)

For all have sinned and fall short of the glory of God, and are justified by his grace as a gift, through the redemption that is in Christ Jesus... (Romans 3:23-24)

TO UNDERSTAND THE IMPORTANCE of ransoms it helps to remember that in the world of the Lord Jesus, around 30% of people were slaves.[1] If you weren't a slave, there was a good chance you owned one. If you didn't, you certainly would have known someone who did. Some people even sold themselves into slavery to pay off their debts. If you were a slave then you could only gain your freedom if someone bought you and set you free. Someone had to redeem you by paying your ransom.

Imagine you were sold into slavery and your brother, who was as poor as you, got a second job and toiled away until he had saved enough to pay the ransom price for one of you. Imagine that he redeemed you and you were set free. His wages paid the cost for your freedom; they were your ransom, your redemption from slavery.

The death of the Lord Jesus achieved our redemption. Scripture declares that we have been set free from the slavery of sin and death so that we may serve the Lord Jesus. Our freedom from our slavery to sin and death did not come cheaply; it came at an unimaginable cost. It came at the cost of the Lord Jesus himself. His death on the cross was the ransom that freed us from our slavery.

You may ask, "If a price was paid to ransom me, then to whom was it paid?" It is not all that clear from my reading of the Bible to whom this ransom was paid. Perhaps we shouldn't push the metaphor too far. The point is not to whom the ransom was paid, but who paid it (and how). And the Bible is clear that it was the Lord Jesus who paid the price, and it was his death that ransomed us from our slavery.

We can see how this works from the Old Testament. When Israel came into the Promised Land, the land was allocated to the Israelites—tribe by tribe, clan by clan, and then to each individual. The land still belonged to God, and each person held the land in trust. The land could not be sold except under the direst of circumstances. This is Naboth's problem when King Ahab of Samaria tries to purchase his vineyard (1 Kings 21). It was very dangerous to say "no" to a king like Ahab, but Naboth was not at liberty to sell his portion of Israel's inheritance in the land of promise.

If in extreme circumstances the land had to be sold, and perhaps the owner also had to be sold as a slave, it was a relative (or "kinsman") who had the responsibility to redeem both him and the land. The kinsman had both the right and the obligation to ransom his relative and his land if he could. If he could not, then the land and the slave's freedom had to be returned every 50 years in the year of jubilee (Leviticus 25:8-34). It was the role of a kinsman to redeem members of the family, and especially to help buy back any land that had been sold for one reason or another.

In the Bible, God is described as a redeemer for his people, Israel. With his mighty hand, he redeemed the Israelites from their slavery to Pharaoh and the Egyptians. But he had to send the ten plagues to do it. It was not as if there was no price to pay. Israel's ransom from slavery came at a cost; something needed to be done to set them free. God did this himself with his "outstretched arm" (Exodus 6:6). God ransomed Israel from her slavery even though he never paid a ransom to anyone.

So it is with the cross. The Lord Jesus redeems us from our slavery to sin and death. He paid the price (Ephesians 1:7), and we can be sure that the death of Jesus was sufficient for all the sins of the world (1 John 2:2).

Slaves are bought and sold. Prisoners of war are sometimes set free upon payment of a ransom. It was a common occurrence at the time of Jesus, and it still happens today. Likewise, we were slaves to sin and death but Jesus' ransom sets us free to serve him (John 8:34-36). In the last book of the Bible, the Lord Jesus is described as having "ransomed people for God from every tribe and language and people and nation" (Revelation 5:9). This is a declaration that the death of Jesus achieved salvation not only for us, but also for a number beyond our imagination. His death was our redemption.

A suggested prayer

Lord Jesus, your death is sufficient for my freedom from sin and death. Help me to trust in your promise without wavering.

ENDNOTE

1. Professor Keith Bradley, 'Resisting Slavery in Ancient Rome', British Broadcasting Corporation, London, 15 October 2010, viewed 16 February 2011: www.bbc.co.uk/history/ancient/romans/slavery_01.shtml

4 | Jesus' death turns away God's anger

My little children, I am writing these things to you so that you may not sin. But if anyone does sin, we have an advocate with the Father, Jesus Christ the righteous. He is the propitiation for our sins, and not for ours only but also for the sins of the whole world. (1 John 2:1-2)

THE WORD TRANSLATED HERE as 'propitiation' is only used twice in the New Testament—here and in 1 John 4:10.[1] Its basic meaning is 'that which turns away anger'—in this case, God's anger. Some people take exception to this idea because they are unhappy about the concept of God's anger. Perhaps this is because they think that God's anger is like ours. Often when we are angry it is because we have lost control over our actions. But God's anger is not like this. He is always in control.

Furthermore, as I have pointed out in the introduction, to do away with God's anger against sin and injustice is to end up with a God who is totally careless about the plight of the world in which we find ourselves. But God is not careless. He is passionate about truth and justice. He loves truth and justice *because he loves people*. He is rightly angered by man's inhumanity to man, and it will not go unpunished.

It's good to know that God is angry at human sin and injustice, because it shows that God cares about the wrongs we suffer. But it's terrible to know that God is angry with you because you sin and treat other people unjustly. And that is what the Bible tells us: that God is angry with each and every one of us (John 3:18; Romans 1:18; 3:9-12, 19-20).

This is why the death of Jesus is so overwhelming. Because the death of the Lord Jesus takes the full punishment for our sins, God's anger is turned aside and he is propitiated (or appeased). The Lord Jesus' substitution for us through bearing our sins turns God's anger aside from us. Because Jesus bore our punishment, he not only set us free from sin and death but also ensured that God is no longer angry with us.

We can see this in the Old Testament. Several times in the Old Testament, God's fierce anger is said to be "turned aside". Because of some action, or some prayer, God does not bring judgement on his people as he said he would, but instead relents and shows mercy (e.g. Exodus 32:11-14; 2 Chronicles 12:12). God's anger is turned aside from Israel by something that someone does.

In the death of the Lord Jesus Christ, God's righteous anger against the sin of the world is obverted. Jesus suffers the wrath of the Father on our behalf, and in his death God's rightful anger is turned aside. By bearing away the sin of the world, Jesus delivers us from having to face God's anger ourselves. Those who trust Jesus will never have to face God's anger.

In case we are tempted to think that bearing away the sin of the world is a small matter, we need to ponder the vastness of the sin of the whole world. Let me give you just one example. I have a friend who lives in Durban, South Africa. He fled the Congo when he was fourteen so he would not be pressed into the children's army. His brother was not so lucky and was forced to fight. At the age of thirteen, he shot a man dead. He is now seventeen and has not spoken since the event.

Who will pay for this terrible mess? Thank goodness God is not careless. We should thank God for being angry at terrible things like this and not just sweeping them under the carpet. This is a small incident in the life of a small nation. Yet incidents just like it are repeated over and over again, all over the world. Aren't you angry when you read this? If not, you are of sterner stuff than I am. I am outraged by it. But the sin against my friend's brother is relatively small in world events. To bear away this sin would require a significant sacrifice, but to bear away the sin of the world required an *enormous* sacrifice.

We can get a glimpse of how much it cost the Lord Jesus by seeing his reaction to his forthcoming death. This is described for us in Matthew's Gospel. Jesus said, "My soul is very sorrowful, even to death" (Matthew 26:38). As Jesus contemplated his death, there is no doubt that he was afraid. He prayed, "My Father, if it be possible, let this cup pass from me; nevertheless, not as I will, but as you will" (Matthew 26:39). Jesus prayed this prayer again and again. The writer to the Hebrews says that he was heard for his godly fear (Hebrews 5:7). The reason Jesus died was not because God did not hear his prayers. Jesus was heard and answered; the answer was "No". There was no other way.

It is possible to romanticize away the horror of the death of the Lord Jesus, but this is not what the Bible does. The Bible does not for a moment minimize it. Jesus was afraid, so he asked his Father if there was any other possible way that we could be saved from God's anger than by Jesus bearing away our sin.

We do well to ponder on this horror, lest we forget at what great price we have been purchased.

A suggested prayer

Lord Jesus, your love overwhelms me. Thank you for turning away God's righteous anger. Help me to love as you love.

ENDNOTE
1. Similar words are used in Romans 3:25 and Hebrews 2:17 and are also translated as 'propitiation'.

5 | Jesus' death brings the defeat of Satan

And you, who were dead in your trespasses and the uncircumcision of your flesh, God made alive together with him, having forgiven us all our trespasses, by cancelling the record of debt that stood against us with its legal demands. This he set aside, nailing it to the cross. He disarmed the rulers and authorities and put them to open shame, by triumphing over them in him. (Colossians 2:13-15)

IN LUKE'S GOSPEL THERE IS an interesting encounter between Jesus and his enemies. Jesus heals a mute man by casting out the demon that was oppressing the man. Jesus is then accused of obtaining his miraculous power from the devil. He explains that his power comes from God and adds, "When a strong man, fully armed, guards his own palace, his goods are safe; but when one stronger than he attacks him and overcomes him, he takes away his armour in which he trusted and divides his spoil" (Luke 11:21-22). In other words, God is stronger than Satan.

Imagine that you and I are fighting, and I overpower you and lock you in a room. You are beating on the door. "Let me out! Let me out!" you cry, but I do not let you out. Then someone else comes along and tells you he will release you. If the door suddenly flies open and you can go free, then you know that this man has managed to get rid of me. You may not know *how* I have been dealt with but you certainly know *that* I have been dealt with.

So it is with Satan. As I pointed out in chapter 3, the death of the Lord Jesus sets us free from our slavery to Satan. This means Satan must have been defeated. The fact that Jesus' death set us free from Satan's power tells us that Satan was defeated by Jesus' death.

On the night before his death, the Lord Jesus described this defeat in the following way:

> "Now is the judgment of this world; now will the ruler of this world be cast out. And I, when I am lifted up from the earth, will draw all people to myself." He said this to show by what kind of death he was going to die. (John 12:31-33)

In the Lord Jesus' mind there is a direct correlation between his death and the overthrow of Satan. Jesus' sin-bearing death is sufficient to secure the overthrow of Satan. By dying for our sins Jesus would draw all people to him, and this would show that Satan had been cast out by that sin-bearing death.

In ancient Rome, a triumph was awarded to any general who won a significant victory. A public holiday would be declared, and the event would be celebrated at the Circus Maximus (a massive Roman stadium used for chariot races). The victorious troop would process into Rome, and at the end of the procession the conquering general would ride in triumph. To his chariot would be shackled the rulers of their enemies. In a very graphic way, this said to even the smallest child watching: so great is the power of Rome that they make slaves of the rulers of their enemies.

The apostle Paul runs with this idea in his letter to the Colossian Christians. In chapter 2 (quoted above), he basically says that Satan was shackled to the Lord Jesus' chariot in his victory procession. The cross was not the sign that the forces of evil had defeated Jesus. It was the sign that Jesus had defeated Satan and publicly exposed him to open shame. It says to those with eyes to see: so great is the death of Jesus that he makes his enemies (and ours) into his slaves.

The death of Jesus was a great victory. And we are the beneficiaries of it. We have been set free.

A suggested prayer

Lord Jesus, your victory over Satan fills me with wonder. Thank you for freeing me from sin and death.

6 | In Jesus' death, the just God justifies sinners freely

But now the righteousness of God has been manifested apart from the law, although the Law and the Prophets bear witness to it—the righteousness of God through faith in Jesus Christ for all who believe. For there is no distinction: for all have sinned and fall short of the glory of God, and are justified by his grace as a gift, through the redemption that is in Christ Jesus, whom God put forward as a propitiation by his blood, to be received by faith. This was to show God's righteousness, because in his divine forbearance he had passed over former sins. It was to show his righteousness at the present time, so that he might be just and the justifier of the one who has faith in Jesus. (Romans 3:21-26)

How can God act justly and yet declare us not guilty when we *are* guilty? This seems an unsolvable dilemma. How can God declare us right with him when we are obviously in the wrong? In Romans 3 (above), Paul argues that it is possible.

He makes the point that all people have sinned. It is clear that our rebellion against God is real and it does matter. Each one of us is God's enemy.

But God has always loved his enemies. We see this

clearly in the Bible, in the little book of Jonah. God instructed Jonah to go to the city of Nineveh and declare that God was going to destroy it (Jonah 1:1-2). Generally, destroying a city is not something one does unless one's enemies inhabit it. The message Jonah was to preach was a clear sign that the Ninevites were God's enemies. Yet Jonah was unwilling to go and preach this message to them (Jonah 1:3). At the end of the book we discover why. Jonah was afraid that if the Ninevites knew of the coming judgement, they would repent and God would show them mercy (Jonah 4:1-3). This is, in fact, what happens (Jonah 3:10, 4:10-11). Jonah found it difficult to come to terms with God's love for his enemies.

God's love moves him to send prophets and preachers to warn his enemies that they are in rebellion against him, giving them a chance to repent. God seeks the repentance and restoration of his enemies and does not rejoice in their death.

But as much as God loves his enemies, he cannot act rightly and at the same time let guilty people go unpunished. And yet the Scriptures make it clear that God declares the guilty in the right with him. How is this possible?

In Romans 3, Paul tells us that this apparent dilemma is resolved in the death of the Lord Jesus Christ for us. He makes the point that, in the matter of sin, there is no difference between Jews and non-Jews. Their rebellion against God may take different forms but it is rebellion nonetheless: "all have sinned". To our astonishment, Paul then says that those same sinners are "justified by his grace" when they trust in Christ Jesus. To be 'justified' is to be declared blameless (an easy way to remember this is to think of it as God treating me 'just-as-if-I'd' never sinned).

Paul's explanation as to how this is possible is simply stated: "God put forward [Christ Jesus] as a propitiation by his blood, to be received by faith".

When we see the Lord Jesus on the cross and hear his terrible agonizing cry, "My God, my God, why have you forsaken me?" (Mark 15:34), we can be in no doubt that God punishes all sin and evil. He was prepared to punish even his own Son when Jesus stood in the place of all sinners. Sin does matter and it doesn't go unpunished. The death of Jesus makes this plain.

However, in the death of the Lord Jesus we are reminded again and again of how much both the Father and the Son love us. The Bible tells us that God loves the world and so he gave his Son. It says that Jesus loves us and so gave his life for us (John 3:16). The sight of Jesus on the cross tells us that God has loved us with an everlasting love (Jeremiah 31:3).

The apostle Paul is gobsmacked by the wonder of this kind of love. He points out that while sometimes people will give their lives for a friend, God showed his love in sending his Son to die for us while we were God's *enemies* (Romans 5:7-8).

What a perfect solution to a seemingly impossible situation.

Recently I read an interview with Dr Greg Clarke, and was particularly impressed by his comment:

> "And to me, it is wonderfully rational—in fact, it's legally supportable—that God would take on himself the cost of justice in the death of Christ, so that the sinner didn't have to pay the debt, and God could extend mercy to the sinner, whilst at the same time being just. That's the genius of Christianity, that God can be just and merciful

at the same time. And I haven't seen in any other religion anything approaching that kind of a solution to the problem of sin."[1]

In the death of the Lord Jesus, God acts rightly in declaring us 'justified'. Because the Lord Jesus was punished in the place of sinners, God's anger was turned from us. With our sins dealt with, and with God's anger propitiated (turned away), God is right in declaring us to be in the right with him. What was not true on the basis of our actions has become true on the basis of Jesus' death, and we receive this justification by faith.

God treats sinners who trust in the Lord Jesus as if they'd never sinned. When you put your trust in the Lord Jesus and receive forgiveness, it is as if you are given a certificate that states: "This is to certify that the bearer has paid the price for all sins". If someone asked, "Where did you get that from?" your answer is clear: "It was given to me by Jesus". The Lord Jesus can do that if he wants to—he alone has earned that right.

Paul sums up his argument by saying, "It was to show his righteousness at the present time, so that he might be just and the justifier of the one who has faith in Jesus". God shows exactly how right he is in declaring us to be right with him. The death of Jesus declares three things:
1. God is just.
2. God punishes sin.
3. God loves sinners.

These wonderful truths all 'kiss' together at the death of the Lord Jesus.

A suggested prayer

Lord Jesus Christ, you alone lived the perfect life and made the perfect sacrifice for us. Your death makes me right with God. Help me to trust my life into your keeping and not to waver in my faith.

ENDNOTE

1. Roland Ashby, 'Love, faith and the new atheism', interview with Dr Greg Clarke, *The Melbourne Anglican*, April 2010.

7 | Jesus' death is the unifying force in the Christian community

Therefore remember that at one time you Gentiles in the flesh, called "the uncircumcision" by what is called the circumcision, which is made in the flesh by hands— remember that you were at that time separated from Christ, alienated from the commonwealth of Israel and strangers to the covenants of promise, having no hope and without God in the world. But now in Christ Jesus you who once were far off have been brought near by the blood of Christ. For he himself is our peace, who has made us both one and has broken down in his flesh the dividing wall of hostility by abolishing the law of commandments expressed in ordinances, that he might create in himself one new man in place of the two, so making peace, and might reconcile us both to God in one body through the cross, thereby killing the hostility. (Ephesians 2:11-16)

And you, who once were alienated and hostile in mind, doing evil deeds, he has now reconciled in his body of flesh by his death, in order to present you holy and blameless and above reproach before him, if indeed you continue in the faith, stable and steadfast, not shifting from the hope of the gospel that you heard, which has been proclaimed in all creation under heaven, and of which I, Paul, became a minister. (Colossians 1:21-23)

ONCE I GRASP THE IDEA THAT I am acceptable to God because of the work of Christ on the cross then this becomes the unifying idea in the fellowship of the people of God. If God accepts me because of the death of Christ then I can expect you to accept me on the same basis. It is not that we are naturally drawn to each other, but that we are made acceptable to each other because of Christ. The apostle Paul argues this in the Ephesians and Colossians passages above. Both the Jew and the non-Jew come to God through Christ and so any barrier (and there had been many) between them is broken down in the death of the Lord Jesus. Each receives the other on an equal footing.

If God says to me "You are acceptable to me because of the work of Jesus on your behalf", and he says the same to you, then you and I must be acceptable to each other on this basis. I must not make other barriers or have 'higher' standards than God does. I must not say to God, "The trouble is that you will fellowship with anyone!" He will say, "I will fellowship with anyone who is in Christ and so should you" (Romans 5:1).

Understanding this truth is wonderfully liberating. We are free to be ourselves. There is no need to pretend. It doesn't matter what you find out about my past, or what I might discover from yours. It is all dealt with in the death of Jesus. That is the basis of acceptability. We are all sinners saved by grace.

The Bible writers also use Christ's sacrifice to encourage us to give ourselves in sacrificial service to each other. The death of the Lord Jesus is an example of Christian service.

Beloved, let us love one another, for love is from God, and whoever loves has been born of God and knows God. Anyone who does not love does not know God, because

God is love. In this the love of God was made manifest among us, that God sent his only Son into the world, so that we might live through him. In this is love, not that we have loved God but that he loved us and sent his Son to be the propitiation for our sins. Beloved, if God so loved us, we also ought to love one another. No-one has ever seen God; if we love one another, God abides in us and his love is perfected in us. (1 John 4:7-12)

Wow—that's a high standard! Yet it is the way God has loved us. This is how God showed his love for us and it becomes the standard for what love really is.

This is no surprise to us. It is exactly the way Jesus told us it would be. At the Last Supper, on the eve of his death, Jesus washed his disciples' feet (John 13:1-20). This was the job of the lowest slave. When Jesus came to Peter, Peter remonstrated. Jesus explained that it was an acted parable of his death. He explained to Peter that while Peter may not have fully understood what Jesus was doing, he would understand later. Jesus concluded this incident by saying that, "If I then, your Lord and Teacher, have washed your feet, you also ought to wash one another's feet" (John 13:14).

There are two things Jesus says to which we must pay attention. The first is that unless we allow Jesus to serve us by bearing away our sins, we cannot belong to him (Mark 10:45). What an insult it is to God to suggest that we are good enough as we are, and that we do not need his forgiveness. What an insult to suggest to God that the death of Jesus was unnecessary in our case. God's assessment of us is very different indeed. The proud-hearted person who refuses to allow Jesus to serve him in this manner cannot be a disciple of the Lord Jesus Christ. Jesus is a true servant king. The cross is Jesus' royal service of each one of us.

The second thing Jesus says is that his death on the cross in humble service to us is an example of the way we should serve each other. It was an example of unqualified humility for us to follow (Philippians 2:1-11). Jesus did not cling to greatness but humbled himself for us. This is therefore how I should behave towards you. The cross is our example of how we should serve each other.

> For the love of Christ controls us, because we have concluded this: that one has died for all, therefore all have died; and he died for all, that those who live might no longer live for themselves but for him who for their sake died and was raised. (2 Corinthians 5:14-15)

We do not naturally do this. Left to our own devices, we are selfish. I think of me first. This, however, is not the way of the cross. There needs to be some radical surgery in my thinking. I am to love as he loved, even when it is inconvenient.

A suggested prayer

Lord Jesus, please flood my heart with your love so that loving others will become my chief delight.

8 | Jesus' death brings forgiveness and cleansing

This is the message we have heard from him and proclaim to you, that God is light, and in him is no darkness at all. If we say we have fellowship with him while we walk in darkness, we lie and do not practice the truth. But if we walk in the light, as he is in the light, we have fellowship with one another, and the blood of Jesus his Son cleanses us from all sin. (1 John 1:5-7)

BECAUSE THE EFFECT OF THE DEATH of Jesus is so great, there are several ways to describe the one reality. To say we're justified is to say that God declares us not guilty. Another way to describe it is to say that we've been cleansed from our sins and forgiven. We no longer carry the guilt of our sin (we've been forgiven); and we no longer bear the stain of our sin (we've been cleansed).

In the passage above, John the apostle tells us that if we confess our sins to God, he "cleanses us from all sin". The verb tense in the original language gives the idea that this cleansing is an ongoing affair. It is as if he is saying, "The blood of Jesus goes on and on cleansing us from all sins".

The prophet Isaiah makes such a promise:

"Come now, let us reason together, says the LORD:

though your sins are like scarlet,
   they shall be as white as snow;
though they are red like crimson,
   they shall become like wool." (Isaiah 1:18)

Isaiah promises that God will cleanse his people's sins so thoroughly that no matter how stained they are by their sin, they will have every last spot and stain removed. There will be no evidence that sin was ever there. The death of Jesus gives us a completely thorough cleansing.

In the last book of the Bible, the apostle John has a vision of heaven. In it he sees a vast multitude of people from every nation under heaven. An elder asks him who they all are. John answers, "Sir, you know". The elder says, "These are the ones coming out of the great tribulation. They have washed their robes and made them white in the blood of the Lamb" (Revelation 7:13-14). This is a graphic way of saying that our sins have been permanently erased. The blood of the Lord Jesus shed on the cross cleanses us completely and permanently from our sins. The death of Jesus gives us a thorough cleansing that makes us permanently clean.

This idea also occurs in the letter to the Colossians:

> And you, who were dead in your trespasses and the uncircumcision of your flesh, God made alive together with him, having forgiven us all our trespasses, by cancelling the record of debt that stood against us with its legal demands. This he set aside, nailing it to the cross. (Colossians 2:13-14)

That word 'cancelled' comes from the root word 'erase'. Such is the death of the Lord Jesus that for those of us who trust in Jesus, the total record of our sins has been erased. Nothing remains. Consequently there can be no condemnation.

This is so comforting. God hasn't turned his anger away and declared us to be in the right, only to leave us to carry a long list of sins and be weighed down by them. He has removed them from the record. The documentation has been torn up. There is nothing there for anyone (including ourselves) to bring up and quote against us.

Sometimes this is described as God forgetting about our past. Jeremiah puts it like this:

> "But this is the covenant that I will make with the house of Israel after those days, declares the LORD: I will put my law within them, and I will write it on their hearts. And I will be their God, and they shall be my people. And no longer shall each one teach his neighbour and each his brother, saying, 'Know the LORD,' for they shall all know me, from the least of them to the greatest, declares the LORD. For I will forgive their iniquity, and I will remember their sin no more." (Jeremiah 31:33-34)

What could be better news than to know that God will remember our sins no more? All this was achieved in the death of the Lord Jesus!

A suggested prayer

Lord Jesus, I stand amazed at the wonder of my sins being forgiven. I am thankful to you for such a gift.

PART II
THE RESURRECTION OF THE LORD JESUS

9 | The facts of the resurrection

THE APOSTLE PAUL TELLS US THAT Jesus died for our sins, was buried, and rose again (1 Corinthians 15:1-11). For hundreds of years, Christians have confessed together in the Apostles' Creed that the Lord Jesus "suffered under Pontius Pilate, was crucified, dead and buried: he descended into hell; the third day he rose again from the dead".

Many have questioned these statements. In fact, Christianity stands or falls on whether or not they are true. We need to look at the facts.

Did Jesus really die?

Does it really matter whether Jesus died on the cross? If Jesus did not die then he did not rise from the dead and Christianity is based on a lie. So we need to be sure that Jesus was in fact dead before he was buried.

Some people have held to the theory that Jesus did not actually die on the cross but was simply unconscious, and that in the cool of the tomb he revived and came out as if he had been resurrected. Others hold to the idea that it was not Jesus who died but another, who replaced him before his death and died in his place.

I have been unable to find any evidence in history at all for either of these theories.

However, it is helpful to see how the Bible writers describe the death of Jesus and how we can be sure that it happened as they record it. The execution of the Lord Jesus was not typical. The trials were hastily convened, and Jesus and those executed with him were nailed to the cross on a Friday. We are told that the Sabbath (Saturday) was a special day of religious significance to the Jews. They did not want the bodies to remain on the crosses on that day so steps were taken to hasten the death of the prisoners (John 19:31-36). When Pilate's soldiers came to Jesus they discovered that he was already dead, so one of soldiers pierced his side with a spear. The apostle John says that he saw "blood and water" flow from the wound. The explanation for this is not clear but the writer is at pains to show that Jesus was in fact dead.

In Mark's Gospel we are told that Joseph, a disciple of Jesus, came and asked Pilate for the body of Jesus so he might bury it. Pilate was surprised that Jesus and the other executed men were already dead, since crucified people often remained on the crosses for days before they died. He spoke to the centurion on duty, who confirmed that Jesus was already dead. Only then did Pilate release the dead body of Jesus to Joseph for burial (Mark 15:42-47). It is highly unlikely that a centurion who regularly oversaw the execution of condemned prisoners would be mistaken as to either the identity of the person crucified, or whether he was really dead.

There can be no reasonable doubt that Jesus died and was buried.

Did Jesus really rise from the dead?

Earlier I mentioned the Apostles' Creed, in which we declare that Jesus "suffered under Pontius Pilate, was crucified, dead and buried ... the third day he rose again from the dead".

It is an astonishing fact that a man should come back to life again from the dead. None of us has any experience that vaguely approximates to this. I know there are people who claim to have had near-death experiences. Please do not think me unkind when I point out that they were all in intensive care! They did not conquer death. They are unlike Jesus, who bounces out of the grave as its great conqueror.

This conquering of death is an absolute necessity if Jesus' death achieved what he claimed it achieved. And, as I pointed out earlier, if Jesus did not rise from the dead then the Christian faith is futile (1 Corinthians 15:17). But people do not normally rise from the dead. The resurrection is such an astonishing event that we need to be convinced of its factual nature.

All four Gospel writers (Matthew, Mark, Luke and John) record events that tell of the resurrection of the Lord Jesus—some in greater detail than others. Mark is content with the empty tomb and the announcement of the angel that Jesus has been raised from the dead (Mark 16:1-7). The other Gospel writers give us much more detail (Matthew 28:1-20; Luke 24:1-49; John 20:1-29).

The apostle Paul tells us of an incident where upward of 500 eyewitnesses see Jesus alive again after his death (1 Corinthians 15:1-8). His appeal is such that he is virtually saying, "Ask anyone in the Jerusalem church. They all saw him."

I am at a total loss as to why anyone would have invented such a story. It is so hard to get people to believe it. What did they have to gain? If Jesus did not rise from the dead, what *did* happen that caused them to describe it in this manner? No other explanation seems plausible except that the disciples—who did not expect Jesus to rise from the dead—became convinced he had risen because of what they saw with their eyes, heard with their ears, and touched with their hands.

Here is a description of one man who was moved from scepticism to belief:

> Now Thomas, one of the Twelve, called the Twin, was not with them when Jesus came. So the other disciples told him, "We have seen the Lord." But he said to them, "Unless I see in his hands the mark of the nails, and place my finger into the mark of the nails, and place my hand into his side, I will never believe."
>
> Eight days later, his disciples were inside again, and Thomas was with them. Although the doors were locked, Jesus came and stood among them and said, "Peace be with you." Then he said to Thomas, "Put your finger here, and see my hands; and put out your hand, and place it in my side. Do not disbelieve, but believe." Thomas answered him, "My Lord and my God!" Jesus said to him, "Have you believed because you have seen me? Blessed are those who have not seen and yet have believed." (John 20:24-29)

Personally, I am pleased we have such an account. Thomas is my sort of man. I am not easily convinced. He is a down-to-earth realist. When the other disciples tell him that they had seen Jesus alive, he is totally unconvinced. It is as if he is saying, "Wake up to yourselves! When you are dead, you are a long time dead." The evidence he thinks he needs is the kind of evidence he is sure he will never see: "Unless I poke my finger into the hole where the nails went in, I will not believe!"

You wouldn't say anything like that if you thought there was a chance it could happen! When I was a child, my father would say to me from time to time, "John, if that ever comes to pass, I'll walk from here to Bathurst on a cold winter's night on my hands without any pants on!" It was his way of saying, "It will never happen". Thomas is saying the same thing: it will never happen. But it did!

What is relatively creepy is that Jesus had heard the conversation although he wasn't there in the flesh! This really is the 'heavy roller' treatment. It is very good evidence indeed. Thomas' reaction to the overwhelming evidence is to move immediately to belief and trust.

Another piece of evidence that has helped me believe in Jesus' resurrection is the total inability of the apostles to revise their ideas on the matter. When the apostle Paul is addressing the Greeks at the Areopagus in Athens and he comes to the resurrection of Jesus, the result is dynamic. Half the place falls about in uncontrollable laughter; the rest shake their heads in unbelief. A few people believe. My experience of preaching the resurrection has been the same. This preaching is really 'bad for business'. Put yourself in the apostles' place. Would you persist in talking about the resurrection under such circumstances, if you weren't convinced that it happened?

If the apostles were not convinced about the truth of the resurrection, they would have filtered it out of their message. But they could not be shaken. They had seen Jesus alive. The event formed their belief, and not the other way around. They were prepared to die, not for what they believed—many have done that—but for the fact that they had seen Jesus alive again.

For me the evidence is overwhelming, and I consider I am not easily persuaded.

We have considered the facts of the resurrection of the Lord Jesus Christ. However, as important as it is to consider *whether* the resurrection took place, we must also consider *why* it took place. In the next few chapters we will consider what the resurrection means.

A suggested prayer

Lord Jesus, I am thankful for the account of Thomas' unbelief. Help me to be one of "those who have not seen and yet have believed".

10 Jesus' resurrection means he is God's king forever

"Let all the house of Israel therefore know for certain that God has made him both Lord and Christ, this Jesus whom you crucified." (Acts 2:36)

SUCH IS THE CONCLUSION THAT Peter reaches in his sermon on the day of Pentecost. He concludes his sermon by stating that Jesus is "both Lord and Christ". To understand the meaning of this phrase we need to look back at the history of God's people.

God had always been Israel's king. He told the Israelites how to live and he fought their battles for them. He used Moses to lead the Israelites as he brought them out of their slavery in Egypt. It was Moses who led them to Sinai, and then through the wilderness, and finally to the brink of entering the Promised Land.

Joshua succeeded Moses as leader, under God. He led the Israelites as they took possession of Canaan, the Promised Land. But after the death of Joshua, Israel had no human leader. So, from time to time, God raised up leaders to rescue the Israelites when they were in strife. These leaders were called the judges. The book of Judges in the Bible finishes with this mournful statement: "In those days there was no king in Israel. Everyone did what was right in his own eyes" (Judges 21:25). Does this mean that they had forgotten that God was their king? I fear it does.

Samuel was the last and in many ways the best of Israel's judges. He was like a second Moses. As Samuel came to the end of his life, Israel asked for a king "like all the nations" around them (1 Samuel 8:5). This was a clear rejection of God as their king, yet God acceded to their request. Saul was anointed as Israel's first king, but he was soon rejected because of his disobedience to God. David replaced Saul as King of Israel, and it was during the reigns of King David and his son Solomon that the monarchy in Israel was really established (around the 11th century BC). Towards the end of David's life, peace was finally established in Israel.

One night during this time of peace, David is walking on the terrace of his palace. He notices that, while he is living in a palace, God is still 'living' in a tent—the 'tent of meeting'. This tent was the place where God met with his people. It was temporary and portable—ideal while Israel was 'on the move'. However, now that Israel is settled in the new land and is politically stable, David decides to build a temple for God. He is encouraged in this by the prophet Nathan. However, God comes to Nathan in a dream with the following instructions:

> "Go and tell my servant David, 'Thus says the LORD: It is not you who will build me a house to dwell in. For I have not lived in a house since the day I brought up Israel to this day, but I have gone from tent to tent and from dwelling to dwelling. In all places where I have moved with all Israel, did I speak a word with any of the judges of Israel, whom I commanded to shepherd my people, saying, "Why have you not built me a house of cedar?"'

Now, therefore, thus shall you say to my servant David, 'Thus says the LORD of hosts, I took you from the pasture, from following the sheep, to be prince over my people Israel, and I have been with you wherever you have gone and have cut off all your enemies from before you. And I will make for you a name, like the name of the great ones of the earth. And I will appoint a place for my people Israel and will plant them, that they may dwell in their own place and be disturbed no more. And violent men shall waste them no more, as formerly, from the time that I appointed judges over my people Israel. And I will subdue all your enemies. Moreover, I declare to you that the LORD will build you a house. When your days are fulfilled to walk with your fathers, I will raise up your offspring after you, one of your own sons, and I will establish his kingdom. He shall build a house for me, and I will establish his throne forever. I will be to him a father, and he shall be to me a son. I will not take my steadfast love from him, as I took it from him who was before you, but I will confirm him in my house and in my kingdom forever, and his throne shall be established forever.'" (1 Chronicles 17:4-14)

God tells David that he is not the person to build the temple. That is for his son Solomon. However, God's instructions contain the most astonishing promise. This promise is important, because it looms large in the history of God's people ever after. The promise is that God's king, in David's line, will rule forever. He is referred to in the Bible as the 'Anointed One', the 'Messiah', and the 'Christ' ('Christ' is a Greek form of the Hebrew 'Messiah'). These are all titles given to God's eternal king.

Psalm 2 is a poem written by David to commemorate this event:

Why do the nations rage
    and the peoples plot in vain?
The kings of the earth set themselves,
    and the rulers take counsel together,
    against the Lord and against his Anointed, saying,
"Let us burst their bonds apart
    and cast away their cords from us."

He who sits in the heavens laughs;
    the Lord holds them in derision.
Then he will speak to them in his wrath,
    and terrify them in his fury, saying,
"As for me, I have set my King
    on Zion, my holy hill."

I will tell of the decree:
The Lord said to me, "You are my Son;
    today I have begotten you.
Ask of me, and I will make the nations your heritage,
    and the ends of the earth your possession.
You shall break them with a rod of iron
    and dash them in pieces like a potter's vessel."

Now therefore, O kings, be wise;
    be warned, O rulers of the earth.
Serve the Lord with fear,
    and rejoice with trembling.
Kiss the Son,
    lest he be angry, and you perish in the way,
    for his wrath is quickly kindled.
Blessed are all who take refuge in him.

In this psalm, God gives the King of Israel absolute power and rule over all the kingdoms of the world. Through this king God will subdue his enemies. He will bring blessing to all those who trust in him. Notice also that God calls the King of Israel his "Son". The term 'Son of God' is another term used in the Bible to describe God's king. It is not to be confused with the term 'God the Son', which is a way of referring to the second person of the Trinity. Both titles are rightly given to the Lord Jesus but they do not both mean the same thing. 'Son of God' is a title given to God's eternal king.

After the reign of Solomon the monarchy in Israel went into decline. Some might say it went into freefall. But what is fascinating is that the promise of the coming Anointed One—the Messiah—was never forgotten. It looms large in the mind of the 8th-century prophet Isaiah. He says that this coming king will bring about universal peace (Isaiah 2:1-5) and usher in the new creation (Isaiah 11). After the fall of Jerusalem (approximately 587BC), God's people were deported to Babylon. There was no longer any King of Israel. However, God's promise was never forgotten.

Around 600 years later, just prior to the birth of the Lord Jesus Christ, the angel Gabriel appeared to Mary the mother of Jesus, and announced that her child would be the promised Messiah. The angel also restated God's promise of eternal rule:

> And the angel said to her, "Do not be afraid, Mary, for you have found favour with God. And behold, you will conceive in your womb and bear a son, and you shall call his name Jesus. He will be great and will be called the Son of the Most High. And the Lord God will give to him the throne of his father David, and he will reign over the house of Jacob forever, and of his kingdom there will be no end." (Luke 1:30-33)

Later in Jesus' life, when he is testing the disciples, he asks them, "Who do you say that I am?" Peter answers, "You are the Christ, the Son of the living God". He is commended for this answer (Matthew 16:13-17). However, when Jesus explains that he is on his way to Jerusalem to die and rise again, Peter objects strenuously. He exclaims, "Far be it from you, Lord! This shall never happen to you" (Matthew 16:22). I don't think Peter is saying, "Dear friend, I cannot bear this idea". He is simply expressing his understanding that the Messiah cannot die, since the Messiah is to reign eternally. The cross shows that Peter was wrong. The Messiah had to die so we would be saved: "Jesus began to show his disciples that he *must* go to Jerusalem and suffer many things from the elders and chief priests and scribes, and be killed, and on the third day be raised" (Matthew 16:21).

When Jesus rose from the dead it was a 'proof' that he was indeed God's Messiah, God's king, whose reign would never end. He is the fulfilment of the long-awaited promise. The apostle Paul describes Jesus like this:

> ...and was declared to be the Son of God in power according to the Spirit of holiness by his resurrection from the dead, Jesus Christ our Lord... (Romans 1:4)

The resurrection of Jesus from the dead declared and confirmed that he was Christ and the Son of God. It was God's public demonstration that his eternal king had taken up his sceptre and sat down on his throne.

In his sermon explaining the Pentecost event, the apostle Peter comes to this conclusion:

"Let all the house of Israel therefore know for certain that God has made him both Lord and Christ, this Jesus whom you crucified." (Acts 2:36)

This is an astonishing thing to claim. Israel had crucified Jesus as a criminal worthy of death. Yet, Peter says, Israel could know "for certain" that God had made Jesus "both Lord and Christ". He argues this from Psalm 16, written by King David:

I have set the LORD always before me;
    because he is at my right hand, I shall not be shaken.

Therefore my heart is glad, and my whole being rejoices;
    my flesh also dwells secure.
For you will not abandon my soul to Sheol,
    or let your holy one see corruption.

You make known to me the path of life;
    in your presence there is fullness of joy;
    at your right hand are pleasures forevermore.
      (Psalm 16:8-11)

Peter's argument is interesting. He insists that Psalm 16 cannot refer to David, since he is dead and buried and his tomb is in Jerusalem. His body did "see corruption"—it decayed. Instead, Psalm 16 refers to the Lord Jesus, whose body did not see corruption. Jesus was raised from the dead and, having died once for our sins, will never die again. His body will never experience decay. And since Jesus will never see corruption, then he is God's "holy one" —God's promised king, the one who is Lord and Christ.

Jesus' resurrection from the dead means we can know for certain that he is now at God's right hand in glory. He is God's king and as such will subdue all God's enemies.

Only people of faith recognize this, but the time will come when Jesus returns and the entire world will see that he is God's king forever.

A suggested prayer

King of glory, I gladly acknowledge you as my king this day. Rule over my life in every way.

11 | Jesus' resurrection means he is the judge of all people

"The times of ignorance God overlooked, but now he commands all people everywhere to repent, because he has fixed a day on which he will judge the world in righteousness by a man whom he has appointed; and of this he has given assurance to all by raising him from the dead." (Acts 17:30-31)

So ARGUES THE APOSTLE PAUL in his sermon at the Areopagus. The resurrection of Jesus from the dead is God's assurance to everyone that Jesus will be the judge of everyone. It is a corollary to the fact that he is God's king. Jesus is God's king and therefore he is the judge of all humanity. The assurance of this is Jesus' resurrection from the dead.

Jesus, himself, had already taught his disciples this truth:

So Jesus said to them, "Truly, truly, I say to you, the Son can do nothing of his own accord, but only what he sees the Father doing. For whatever the Father does, that the Son does likewise. For the Father loves the Son and shows him all that he himself is doing. And greater works than these will he show him, so that you may marvel. For as the Father raises the dead and gives them life, so also the Son gives life to whom he will. The Father judges no-one, but has given all judgment to the Son, that all may honour the Son, just as they honour the Father. Whoever does not honour the Son does not honour the Father who sent him. Truly, truly, I say to you, whoever hears my word and believes him who sent me has eternal life. He does not come into judgment, but has passed from death to life.

"Truly, truly, I say to you, an hour is coming, and is now here, when the dead will hear the voice of the Son of God, and those who hear will live. For as the Father has life in himself, so he has granted the Son also to have life in himself. And he has given him authority to execute judgment, because he is the Son of Man. Do not marvel at this, for an hour is coming when all who are in the tombs will hear his voice and come out, those who have done good to the resurrection of life, and those who have done evil to the resurrection of judgment.

"I can do nothing on my own. As I hear, I judge, and my judgment is just, because I seek not my own will but the will of him who sent me." (John 5:19-30)

At the close of the age in the final judgement it will be the Lord Jesus who will separate the sheep from the goats (Matthew 25:31-46). The Father has given all judgement into the Son's hands. The Son of God is also God the Son —the one who does everything that the Father does. Just as the Father has life in himself and is a source of life, so the Son gives life to those who hear his word and put their faith in him. And just as he brings life to the believing dead, so he also brings judgement to the unbelieving dead. Jesus executes the Father's judgement on everyone—for eternal life or eternal punishment.

It is a great relief to know what will happen on that judgement day. We know the sort of questions that God will ask us. Strange as it may be, he will not ask the question, "Have you lived a good life?" We know the answer to that! Thankfully, it is irrelevant. No, the questions will swing on the person of the Lord Jesus Christ. "Did you acknowledge him as your king?" That's the burning question (2 Thessalonians 1:8-10). "Whose side were you on?" "Were you a loyal follower or still a rebel?"

Jesus' judgement is final. We might wish that it were otherwise, but the Bible gives us no indication that this is so. It must be this way—otherwise there would be rebels in the new creation. And how can the new creation contain rebels? It would turn out just like the present one.

Because of the certainty of this judgement day, we are commanded by God to repent and acknowledge Jesus as rightful ruler over us, so that the judgement day will not catch us 'on the hop'.

We would be wise to do so. Jesus has risen from the dead. He is the judge.

A suggested prayer

Lord Jesus, I thank you that your death is sufficient for my forgiveness and that I will not be overthrown on that great judgement day. Thank you for showing me this by your resurrection from the dead.

12 | Jesus' resurrection means his sacrifice was full, perfect and sufficient

My little children, I am writing these things to you so that you may not sin. But if anyone does sin, we have an advocate with the Father, Jesus Christ the righteous. He is the propitiation for our sins, and not for ours only but also for the sins of the whole world. (1 John 2:1-2)

IN THE ANGLICAN COMMUNION service, the death of the Lord Jesus is described as "a full, perfect, and sufficient sacrifice, oblation, and satisfaction, for the sins of the whole world". This sounds wonderful! But is there any real proof that this is so? Can I be sure that the death of Jesus will secure my permanent forgiveness?

In the Bible, the result of sin is always death (Romans 6:23). This, of course, must be the case, since God is the source of life. Sin causes me to rebel against God and consequently to be separated from God. As God is life, separation from God is separation from life. To separate myself from him in sin is to invite death as a natural consequence.

If Jesus has indeed paid the full penalty for sin, then we would expect to see the end of death. That is life. In fact that is exactly what we do see. The resurrection of Jesus shows that he is the conqueror of death and that he has paid the full price for our sins. So sure of this is the apostle Paul that he is able to say:

> And if Christ has not been raised, your faith is futile and you are still in your sins. Then those also who have fallen asleep in Christ have perished. If in Christ we have hope in this life only, we are of all people most to be pitied.
>
> But in fact Christ has been raised from the dead, the firstfruits of those who have fallen asleep. (1 Corinthians 15:17-20)

If Christ is not raised from the dead then he has not borne away the sin of the world. Death still holds sway. But this is not the case. Christ's resurrection from the dead tells us that his death freed us from sin and death.

Because of the resurrection of Jesus Christ from the dead, we can be certain that his death on the cross was indeed "a full, perfect, and sufficient sacrifice, oblation, and satisfaction, for the sins of the whole world"—yours, mine, and more! It is a source of endless thanksgiving.

A suggested prayer

Lord Jesus Christ, your victory over sin and death is the cause of endless joy to me. Thank you for doing this on my behalf, and demonstrating it through your resurrection from the dead.

13 | Jesus' resurrection removes our fear of death

I tell you this, brothers: flesh and blood cannot inherit the kingdom of God, nor does the perishable inherit the imperishable. Behold! I tell you a mystery. We shall not all sleep, but we shall all be changed, in a moment, in the twinkling of an eye, at the last trumpet. For the trumpet will sound, and the dead will be raised imperishable, and we shall be changed. For this perishable body must put on the imperishable, and this mortal body must put on immortality. When the perishable puts on the imperishable, and the mortal puts on immortality, then shall come to pass the saying that is written:

"Death is swallowed up in victory."
"O death, where is your victory?
O death, where is your sting?"

The sting of death is sin, and the power of sin is the law. But thanks be to God, who gives us the victory through our Lord Jesus Christ.

Therefore, my beloved brothers, be steadfast, immovable, always abounding in the work of the Lord, knowing that in the Lord your labour is not in vain. (1 Corinthians 15:50-58)

MOST PEOPLE I KNOW ARE frightened about death. If you wish to bring a dinner conversation to a crashing, grinding halt, whisper to your hostess, "Have you given much thought to your death lately?" You probably won't be invited back again. You will probably be struck off the Christmas card list. People are so afraid of death that they don't wish to discuss it at all.

Why is this so? Is it because death is unknown? Is it because death has such power over us? Neither is true.

In the passage above, Paul is claiming that death gets its power through our disobedience to the law. But the Lord Jesus has fully kept the law on our behalf. He has taken away the power of death by bearing our sins. We no longer die as though imprisoned in death's power, lost and without hope. We die in the certain hope of our resurrection from the dead because Jesus has redeemed us from our slavery to death. He did this by taking the punishment our sins deserved, and then he rose from the dead. The death of Jesus breaks the power of sin and death. The resurrection of Jesus from the dead shows us that death's power is finished. There is no need for us to fear death's power any longer.

Jesus died and rose from the dead. Jesus has been there before us. There is nothing to be frightened of. He knows the way. I don't know anyone else who can offer you that security.

> Simon Peter said to him, "Lord, where are you going?" Jesus answered him, "Where I am going you cannot follow me now, but you will follow afterward." Peter said to him, "Lord, why can I not follow you now? I will lay down my life for you." Jesus answered, "Will you lay down your life for me? Truly, truly, I say to you, the rooster will not crow till you have denied me three times.

"Let not your hearts be troubled. Believe in God; believe also in me. In my Father's house are many rooms. If it were not so, would I have told you that I go to prepare a place for you? And if I go and prepare a place for you, I will come again and will take you to myself, that where I am you may be also. And you know the way to where I am going." Thomas said to him, "Lord, we do not know where you are going. How can we know the way?" Jesus said to him, "I am the way, and the truth, and the life. No one comes to the Father except through me. If you had known me, you would have known my Father also. From now on you do know him and have seen him." (John 13:36-14:7)

Those who are in Christ have had their fear of death removed. It is as if Jesus is saying, "Trust me, I know the way. I've been there before."

The fear of death is a terrible power that blights our lives. Fear of death stopped even Peter from following his Lord and Master. Fear of death prompted him to deny Jesus three separate times. The fear of death can lead us to do all sorts of wrong and evil things.

But Jesus tells us not to fear, not to let our hearts be troubled. He has gone before us. He has walked the path of death that we too must walk, if he does not return first. And he has risen again to tell us that we do not need to fear. His death and resurrection has created a home for us, a place for us, to which he will take us when he returns.

Jesus has conquered the grave, and can show us the way through it and into an everlasting life.

A suggested prayer

Lord Jesus, thank you for taking away my fear of death. Thank you that I can trust myself to you in that hour.

14 | Jesus' resurrection means we too will have resurrection bodies

"Truly, truly, I say to you, whoever hears my word and believes him who sent me has eternal life. He does not come into judgement, but has passed from death to life.

"Truly, truly, I say to you, an hour is coming, and is now here, when the dead will hear the voice of the Son of God, and those who hear will live. For as the Father has life in himself, so he has granted the Son also to have life in himself. And he has given him authority to execute judgment, because he is the Son of Man." (John 5:24-27)

I GREW UP IN A CONGREGATION where people often talked about "going to heaven". However, the Bible is much more preoccupied with the new creation and our place in it with our resurrection bodies. Jesus himself taught us that we would have resurrection bodies. He declared that when we believe his word—his teaching about himself—we immediately pass from death to life without end. We will never face judgement. Jesus says that one day he will speak again and, when that word is spoken, those who believed his teaching will hear his voice and live again, and live forever. In saying this, Jesus teaches us that we will have resurrection bodies. He is speaking of the resurrection of the dead.

Paul also teaches us that we will have resurrection bodies. He states that our bodies will be recognizable but, unlike our earthly bodies, they will be appropriate for the new creation:

> But someone will ask, "How are the dead raised? With what kind of body do they come?" You foolish person! What you sow does not come to life unless it dies. And what you sow is not the body that is to be, but a bare kernel, perhaps of wheat or of some other grain. But God gives it a body as he has chosen, and to each kind of seed its own body. For not all flesh is the same, but there is one kind for humans, another for animals, another for birds, and another for fish. There are heavenly bodies and earthly bodies, but the glory of the heavenly is of one kind, and the glory of the earthly is of another. There is one glory of the sun, and another glory of the moon, and another glory of the stars; for star differs from star in glory.
>
> So is it with the resurrection of the dead. What is sown is perishable; what is raised is imperishable. It is sown in dishonour; it is raised in glory. It is sown in weakness; it is raised in power. It is sown a natural body; it is raised a spiritual body. If there is a natural body, there is also a spiritual body. (1 Corinthians 15:35-44)

Our resurrection bodies will be *our* bodies—just as they are our bodies now. The body that is sown is the body that will be raised; it is the same body that will be raised. But our resurrection bodies will be changed to fit the new creation and all its glory. They will not be mortal, they will not be perishable, they will not be weak and dishonoured, and they will not be natural. These are all things that our bodies are now, things that make them appropriate for living in the world God has created. But Christ will take them up and transform them so that they will be breathtaking! They will be immortal, imperishable, powerful, glorious, and spiritual. They will be perfectly suited to the new creation.

> Then I saw a new heaven and a new earth, for the first heaven and the first earth had passed away, and the sea was no more. And I saw the holy city, new Jerusalem, coming down out of heaven from God, prepared as a bride adorned for her husband. And I heard a loud voice from the throne saying, "Behold, the dwelling place of God is with man. He will dwell with them, and they will be his people, and God himself will be with them as their God. He will wipe away every tear from their eyes, and death shall be no more, neither shall there be mourning, nor crying, nor pain any more, for the former things have passed away."
>
> And he who was seated on the throne said, "Behold, I am making all things new." Also he said, "Write this down, for these words are trustworthy and true." (Revelation 21:1-5)

This will be a new world where there is no sickness, no death, no grief or sorrow, no suffering—nothing that blights and eats away at human life. Evil will have no place; everything will be in perfect harmony. It will be a world more glorious, spiritual, and filled with the power of God than this current world. And the bodies with which we will be raised will be in perfect harmony with this new world. We will have resurrection bodies that will live perfectly in the new creation.

I personally find this very satisfying. When I think of my friends who have died, I find it difficult to think of them as disembodied spirits. That is not how I knew them. It is not how I related to them. But when I see the apostles relating to the risen Lord Jesus, I can see how it will be. I can see that the resurrection of the Lord Jesus means that there really is eternal life; there really is a new world in which we will live and relate to each other and to the Lord Jesus.

A suggested prayer
Glorious Lord Jesus, your own resurrection assures me that I too will have a resurrection body. I thank you for this.

15 | Jesus' resurrection means he alone can take us through death to life eternal

"Fear not, I am the first and the last, and the living one. I died, and behold I am alive forevermore, and I have the keys of Death and Hades." (Revelation 1:17-18)

I KNOW NO-ONE WHO HAS DIED and risen from the grave except Jesus. Jesus leaps from his grave as the great conqueror of death. That is true of no-one else. When we say that someone is 'dead and buried', it is a sign that they will never act again. We do not expect people to come back to life once they have died. What Jesus did, in rising from the grave and conquering death, is completely unprecedented. It makes him uniquely qualified to take us through death.

I am always interested in people's credentials, especially when I am asked to trust my life to them. Since Jesus is the only person who has been through death and come 'up' the other side, he is the one I will trust with my life. I know nothing about my own death. I don't even know when it will happen. I know very little about entry into eternity. But Jesus knows about all of these, and he is the one I will trust.

On several occasions, friends in London have invited me to dinner. They have sometimes taken me to their club. These clubs always seem to have enormous doormen dressed in dinner jackets. As I approach the door, the doorman steps in my way. "Are you a member here, sir?" My host says quickly, "It's all right, Charles, he's with me". It works like a charm and gets me in every time. "You are very welcome, sir. I hope you enjoy yourself." It never fails.

Can you think of anything better than to arrive into eternity with the Lord Jesus saying, "It's all right, he's with me"? It always matters who you know rather than what you know. A recommendation from the Lord Jesus will be sufficient. Death and Hades will step back, open their doors and say, "Very good, Lord, pass this way." They will not be our jailers; they will be our doormen as we pass them by.

Jesus, and Jesus alone, has died and risen from the dead. He's been through death and so he knows the way. He has conquered death and so he has the right to usher you and I through its doors and into eternal life. Jesus is well qualified to take us through death and into eternal life because of his resurrection from the grave.

A suggested prayer

Gracious Lord Jesus, your own resurrection declares that you are able to take me through death and into eternal life. Teach me to not be afraid of death's embrace.

PART III
THE DEATH AND RESURRECTION AS A PATTERN

16 | The pattern of all future judgement

Such is the nature of God's sovereign rule over his world that the psalmist is able to say:

> Surely the wrath of man shall praise you;
>> the remnant of wrath you will put on like a belt.
>> (Psalm 76:10)

It seems so strange to us that God should be praised when men are doing evil. But in the Bible, that is exactly what happens.

The life of the patriarch Joseph is a good example. He is the favourite of his father and disliked by his elder brothers. They decide to kill him but, as opportunity arises, they sell him into slavery. He ends up in Egypt. After many misfortunes he ends up as prime minister of Egypt. Because of Joseph's careful stewardship, there is grain in Egypt when the neighbouring countries are in famine. Joseph's brothers are sent by their father to Egypt to buy grain. They do not recognize Joseph their brother. You might have expected him to wreak vengeance on them. However, he says to his brothers, "You meant evil against me, but God meant it for good" (Genesis 50:20). Their actions were evil, but God was using them to bring his purposes to pass. Joseph praises God for the way he used the sinfulness of Joseph's brothers to bring about good.

This is the Bible's way of speaking about God's relationship to human evil. God uses our evil for good, and this brings praise to God.

You might ask me, "How can the war in the Middle East bring praise to God?" I don't know the answer to that specific question, but it will be like the death and resurrection of the Lord Jesus. If we had been on the Good Friday side of this event and we had seen Jesus nailed to the cross, we would have been crying out, "Stop this! Why doesn't God do something about it?" However when we got to Easter Sunday, we'd be astonished. With our mouths hanging open, we'd whisper, "Who would have believed it could have happened like that?"

In his sermon on Pentecost Day just after the Holy Spirit had been given to the apostles, Peter proclaims God's sovereign power:

> "Men of Israel, hear these words: Jesus of Nazareth, a man attested to you by God with mighty works and wonders and signs that God did through him in your midst, as you yourselves know—this Jesus, delivered up according to the definite plan and foreknowledge of God, you crucified and killed by the hands of lawless men. God raised him up, loosing the pangs of death, because it was not possible for him to be held by it. For David says concerning him,
>
>> "'I saw the Lord always before me,
>>   for he is at my right hand that I may not be shaken;
>> therefore my heart was glad, and my tongue rejoiced;
>>   my flesh also will dwell in hope.
>> For you will not abandon my soul to Hades,
>>   or let your Holy One see corruption.
>> You have made known to me the paths of life;
>>   you will make me full of gladness with your presence.'

"Brothers, I may say to you with confidence about the patriarch David that he both died and was buried, and his tomb is with us to this day. Being therefore a prophet, and knowing that God had sworn with an oath to him that he would set one of his descendants on his throne, he foresaw and spoke about the resurrection of the Christ, that he was not abandoned to Hades, nor did his flesh see corruption. This Jesus God raised up, and of that we all are witnesses. Being therefore exalted at the right hand of God, and having received from the Father the promise of the Holy Spirit, he has poured out this that you yourselves are seeing and hearing. For David did not ascend into the heavens, but he himself says,

> "'The Lord said to my Lord,
> Sit at my right hand,
> until I make your enemies your footstool.'

Let all the house of Israel therefore know for certain that God has made him both Lord and Christ, this Jesus whom you crucified." (Acts 2:22-36)

Jesus was a man for whom God himself had shown his unprecedented approval through all the works, wonders and signs God did through him. His crucifixion was a travesty of justice. It stood truth and right on its head, and it was the work of lawless men. It was evil.

And yet, as Peter points out, God was using this evil to his glory. What men intended for evil, God used for good. What happened on the cross occurred according to God's foreknowledge and definite plan. Its evil served God's purposes. By dying, Jesus paid the penalty for our sin, and so our sins have been dealt with. Death was unable to maintain its hold on Jesus. God raised him up and thus death was defeated, its pangs forevermore loosened. God exalted Jesus to his own right hand and so made it clear to us all that Jesus is God's Christ, and Lord of all. And from the Father's right hand, the Lord Jesus has received the Holy Spirit promised by the Old Testament prophets and has poured the Spirit out upon his followers—on those who place their faith in him and in his death and resurrection.

So much good from so much evil! God used this evil act to save the world. Peter shows us that the cross brings glory to God.

On the judgement day all evil will be like that. In our disobedience we thumb our nose at God, yet he will use it for his glory. It really is good!

A suggested prayer

Were the whole realm of nature mine
That were an offering far too small
Love so amazing so divine
Demands my life, my soul, my all.[1]

ENDNOTE

1. From Isaac Watts' hymn, 'When I Survey the Wondrous Cross', 1707.

17 | The pattern of the Christian experience

THE BIBLE NOT ONLY DESCRIBES the beneficial effects of the death and resurrection of the Lord Jesus Christ, but also shows it to be the pattern for the true Christian experience.

Christians have died to an old way of life, which was marked by rebellion and indifference to God, and have been raised to a new way of life marked by obedience to Jesus as Lord and Saviour. The death of Jesus on the cross makes it impossible to live the old way any longer.

Let me explain it like this. Imagine that a book was written entitled *John Chapman Runs his Own Life*. It finished something like this:

> As he contemplated the death of the Lord Jesus Christ on the cross, John Chapman began to realize that there was no other way he could get right with God, except through faith in the Lord Jesus and what he had done. The death of Jesus had caused 'death' to any other way to get right with God.
>
> John Chapman put his trust in the Lord Jesus, and with that, he died.
>
> The end

At exactly the same time, a new volume of John Chapman's life began. That book is entitled *John Chapman Tries to Obey Jesus his Lord*, and it is still being written. It begins like this:

At age 17, John Chapman died to an old way of life and was born again into a new way of life (John 3:3). In this new life he was greatly helped by God's Spirit, the Spirit of the Lord Jesus Christ, who lived within him urging him to obey the Lord Jesus Christ...

The difference between these two ways of life is like the death and resurrection of Jesus. As he died and was raised again, so we have died to one way of life and been raised to a new way of life.

As the old life had rules to live by, so does the new. Let me draw your attention to a part of the New Testament that describes this:

> For through the law I died to the law, so that I might live to God. I have been crucified with Christ. It is no longer I who live, but Christ who lives in me. And the life I now live in the flesh I live by faith in the Son of God, who loved me and gave himself for me. I do not nullify the grace of God, for if righteousness were through the law, then Christ died for no purpose. (Galatians 2:19-21)

The Galatian Christians had heard the gospel and put their trust in the Lord Jesus. New teachers arrived and undermined their confidence in what they had done. These new teachers suggested that as well as trusting in the Lord Jesus, they had to keep the laws of Moses. But Paul could see that if anything had to be added to the work of the Lord Jesus then this automatically made his work defective and his sacrifice insufficient.

In the algebra of salvation:

$$Jesus^+ = Jesus^-$$

To add anything to Jesus' death and resurrection—to say that we need to do something as well as trusting him and his sacrifice—is to take away from Jesus and his death.

Do I need to do certain things as well as trust in Jesus and his death for our sins? "No, indeed", says the apostle. "I have been crucified with Christ." Of course he wasn't on the cross with the Lord Jesus, but what he is saying is that when Christ died on the cross, he made an end of all other ways to get right with God. Paul says, "I died to the law as a way of getting right with God". As far as the law was concerned, Paul was a dead man. The law had no claims upon him any more.

In the first general election held in Australia after my mother died, she received a summons to show why she should not be fined for not voting (since voting is compulsory in Australia). I answered on her behalf: "My mother is dead and doesn't vote in general elections any more." You see, she was beyond the reach of the law. The law is only for the living.

Paul is saying that when Christ died, Paul also died. Having died, the law had no claim on him and could no longer stand between him and God. There was no other way, now, than to trust Christ's sacrifice alone to make him right with God. He had died to a way of life where he tried to win God's favour. It was not the right way. Only the death of Jesus could do that.

However, Paul's death was not the end. He had been raised to a new way of life: "It is no longer I who live, but Christ who lives in me. And the life I now live in the flesh I live by faith in the Son of God, who loved me and gave himself for me" (Galatians 2:20). And just as there was behaviour that typified the old way of life, so there is behaviour that typifies the new way of life. Paul describes this in Colossians:

If then you have been raised with Christ, seek the things that are above, where Christ is, seated at the right hand of God. Set your minds on things that are above, not on things that are on earth. For you have died, and your life is hidden with Christ in God. When Christ who is your life appears, then you also will appear with him in glory.

Put to death therefore what is earthly in you: sexual immorality, impurity, passion, evil desire, and covetousness, which is idolatry. On account of these the wrath of God is coming. In these you too once walked, when you were living in them. But now you must put them all away: anger, wrath, malice, slander, and obscene talk from your mouth. Do not lie to one another, seeing that you have put off the old self with its practices and have put on the new self, which is being renewed in knowledge after the image of its creator. Here there is not Greek and Jew, circumcised and uncircumcised, barbarian, Scythian, slave, free; but Christ is all, and in all.

Put on then, as God's chosen ones, holy and beloved, compassionate hearts, kindness, humility, meekness, and patience, bearing with one another and, if one has a complaint against another, forgiving each other; as the Lord has forgiven you, so you also must forgive. And above all these put on love, which binds everything together in perfect harmony. And let the peace of Christ rule in your hearts, to which indeed you were called in one body. And be thankful. Let the word of Christ dwell in you richly, teaching and admonishing one another in all wisdom, singing psalms and hymns and spiritual songs, with thankfulness in your hearts to God. And whatever you do, in word or deed, do everything in the name of the Lord Jesus, giving thanks to God the Father through him. (Colossians 3:1-17)

Paul explains that now we have been raised to a new life, we are to live appropriately. Do you notice the behaviour that was typical of the old way of life? Sexual immorality, impurity, passion, evil desire, covetousness and idolatry… such behaviour is totally inappropriate for the resurrection life. It is not, I am sorry to say, impossible to act in these ways in the new way of life, but it is totally inappropriate, so we should not do so. "Put them to death", the Bible says. This means we need to renounce these kinds of behaviour, being ruthless and self-disciplined about sin. We need to fight against these things in our lives and persevere in trying to eradicate them, no matter how often we suffer setbacks. The new way of life involves an ongoing death to the behaviours of the old way of life.

Please note what *is* appropriate to the new way of life: compassion, kindness, humility, meekness, patience, forbearance, forgiveness and love. These are to be practised until they are second nature to us. These are the behaviours that describe Jesus himself; this is a call to be Christlike. God himself is at work in us to make us like Christ. It is a lifelong process, but the goal is a great miracle—we will be like Christ himself. The process will be completed only when Christ returns. At this present time our lives are hidden with Christ in God, but when Christ appears then you and I will appear with him, clothed in the same glory that he has. We will be like him. But throughout our lives we are to practise these qualities, even as God changes us to make us more like Christ. Knowing this goal, we never give up.

I suppose the classic illustration of the 'death-resurrection' experience of the Christian is found in Romans 6:

What shall we say then? Are we to continue in sin that grace may abound? By no means! How can we who died to sin still live in it? Do you not know that all of us who have been baptized into Christ Jesus were baptized into his death? We were buried therefore with him by baptism into death, in order that, just as Christ was raised from the dead by the glory of the Father, we too might walk in newness of life.

For if we have been united with him in a death like his, we shall certainly be united with him in a resurrection like his. We know that our old self was crucified with him in order that the body of sin might be brought to nothing, so that we would no longer be enslaved to sin. For one who has died has been set free from sin. Now if we have died with Christ, we believe that we will also live with him. We know that Christ, being raised from the dead, will never die again; death no longer has dominion over him. For the death he died he died to sin, once for all, but the life he lives he lives to God. So you also must consider yourselves dead to sin and alive to God in Christ Jesus.

Let not sin therefore reign in your mortal body, to make you obey its passions. Do not present your members to sin as instruments for unrighteousness, but present yourselves to God as those who have been brought from death to life, and your members to God as instruments for righteousness. For sin will have no dominion over you, since you are not under law but under grace. (Romans 6:1-14)

When we became Christians (that is, when we were baptized into Christ's death), we died to an old way of life and were raised to a new way.

Just as Christ died to the penalty of sin, we too should see that there is no punishment for our sins because

Christ has taken it on the cross. We have died to the punishment and so we are to live a new life dominated not by sin, which is inappropriate, but by God-honouring behaviour, which is appropriate for this resurrection life.

While you are waiting to take your place in the new creation, make the most of the death and resurrection of Christ here and now. Live the resurrection life for all it is worth.

A suggested prayer

Lord Jesus, thank you for bringing my old life to an end. Please make me more like you.

Feedback on this resource

We really appreciate getting feedback about our resources—not just suggestions for how to improve them, but also positive feedback and ways they can be used. We especially love to hear that the resources may have helped someone in their Christian growth.

You can send feedback to us via the 'Feedback' menu in our online store, or write to us at PO Box 225, Kingsford NSW 2032, Australia.

matthiasmedia

Matthias Media is an evangelical publishing ministry that seeks to persuade all Christians of the truth of God's purposes in Jesus Christ as revealed in the Bible, and equip them with high-quality resources, so that by the work of the Holy Spirit they will:

- abandon their lives to the honour and service of Christ in daily holiness and decision-making
- pray constantly in Christ's name for the fruitfulness and growth of his gospel
- speak the Bible's life-changing word whenever and however they can— in the home, in the world and in the fellowship of his people.

It was in 1988 that we first started pursuing this mission, and in God's kindness we now have more than 300 different ministry resources being used all over the world. These resources range from Bible studies and books through to training courses and audio sermons.

To find out more about our large range of very useful resources, and to access samples and free downloads, visit our website:

www.matthiasmedia.com.au

How to buy our resources

1. Direct from us over the internet:
   – in the US: www.matthiasmedia.com
   – in Australia and the rest of the world:
     www.matthiasmedia.com.au

2. Direct from us by phone:
   – in the US: 1 866 407 4530
   – in Australia: 1800 814 360
     (Sydney: 9663 1478)
   – international: +61-2-9663-1478

Register at our website for our **free** regular email update to receive information about the latest new resources, **exclusive special offers**, and free articles to help you grow in your Christian life and ministry.

3. Through a range of outlets in various parts of the world. Visit **www.matthiasmedia.com.au/information/contact-us** for details about recommended retailers in your part of the world, including www.thegoodbook.co.uk in the United Kingdom.

4. Trade enquiries can be addressed to:
   – in the US and Canada: sales@matthiasmedia.com
   – in Australia and the rest of the world: sales@matthiasmedia.com.au

Also by John Chapman

Making the Most of the Rest of Your Life

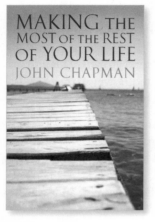

The Bible teaches that all people will die, and all will survive the grave and live either *with* Christ or *without* him in eternity. 76-year-old evangelist John Chapman explores how we can know if this is true, and, if so, how to prepare for that eternity. This is a warm-hearted, good-humoured and challenging evangelistic book for 'seniors'. It explains how we can know about life after death, what the new creation will be like, and whether we can be sure of being part of it. (Large print!)

On this short DVD, well-known Bible teachers John Chapman and Tony Payne talk through the ideas in the book. It is an ideal alternative to the book for those who are less likely to read but more likely to watch an engaging discussion on TV.

Run time: 22 minutes

FOR MORE INFORMATION OR TO ORDER CONTACT:

Matthias Media
Ph: +61-2-9663-1478
Fax: +61-2-9663-3265
Email: sales@matthiasmedia.com.au
www.matthiasmedia.com.au

Matthias Media (USA)
Ph: 1-866-407-4530
Fax: 330-953-1712
Email: sales@matthiasmedia.com
www.matthiasmedia.com

Also by John Chapman

A Fresh Start

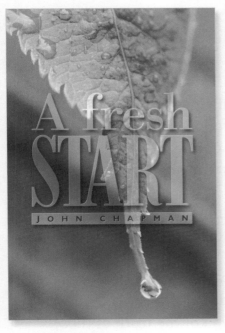

Something is terribly wrong—with our world, with our relationships, with us. We all sense this at different times. But is there anything that can be done about it?

With all the honesty and humour for which he is famous, John Chapman tells us in *A Fresh Start* that God has done something about it. We read about:

- what God has done for us through his Son, Jesus
- how we can know it is true
- what the alternatives are
- what we should do about it.

If you have been searching for a book that simply and clearly explains what it means to be a Christian, either for your own or another's benefit, your search is over.

FOR MORE INFORMATION OR TO ORDER CONTACT:

Matthias Media
Ph: +61-2-9663-1478
Fax: +61-2-9663-3265
Email: sales@matthiasmedia.com.au
www.matthiasmedia.com.au

Matthias Media (USA)
Ph: 1-866-407-4530
Fax: 330-953-1712
Email: sales@matthiasmedia.com
www.matthiasmedia.com

Also from Matthias Media

Right Side Up

"I set out to write a book for new Christians, to explain what it means to be a Christian and what the lifelong adventure of following Jesus is like. But I soon realized that what Jesus wants to say to a new Christian is really the same thing he wants to keep saying to the seasoned saint: "Whoever loses his life for my sake will find it". My prayer is that this book will persuade you of the truth of those words, and help you live like you believe them. It's a book for the brand new Christian that should challenge every believer—whether you've been following Jesus for five minutes or fifty years."—Author, Paul Grimmond

FOR MORE INFORMATION OR TO ORDER CONTACT:

Matthias Media
Ph: +61-2-9663-1478
Fax: +61-2-9663-3265
Email: sales@matthiasmedia.com.au
www.matthiasmedia.com.au

Matthias Media (USA)
Ph: 1-866-407-4530
Fax: 330-953-1712
Email: sales@matthiasmedia.com
www.matthiasmedia.com